Create the life
you want to

A Season Of Change

A SEASON OF CHANGE

Ryan Lamont Jones

Foreword by
Karen Newman Jones

Copyright © July 2017 by Ryan Lamont Jones

All rights reserved. No part of this book may be reproduced or transmitted in any form or by any means, electronic or mechanical, including photocopying, recording or by any information storage and retrieval system, without permission in writing from the copyright owner.

Email: ryan@rljonesandassociates.net
Website: www.rljonesandassociates.net

ISBN-13:978-1541141032
ISBN-10:1541141032

~DEDICATION~

These people have poured into my life and kept (and keep) me humble. This book is dedicated to the following people:

Karen Newman Jones (my beautiful and supportive wife), thank you for never giving up on me and challenging me to achieve greatness. I am grateful for all of your prayers and unconditional love. I love you.

Morgan Denise, Omar Julian, Nigel Ryan and Rhyann Louise (our children); Aiden Deon (our grandson) and Deon Wilson (our son-in-love), thank you for your love and support and making me proud to be your father.

Dorothy S. Godbold and Corinthia B. Hankins (my grandmothers) and to all of my other family members.

Kim Hawthorne: Thank you for your "Wisdom Words." I truly believe there is a Divine reason we connected. I appreciate you "having my back" and know that I have yours as well.

Mark Christopher Lawrence: Thank you for being a true brother. You are truly a blessing for "bringing the funny." I am glad to be "stuck with you."

Jazsmin Lewis: Thank you for being a light in my life. You are truly an amazing "sister" with a heart of love. I "hope to be like you" and light up a room every time I enter.

~CONTENT~

A Season of Change	1
The Power of 'I Am'	3
The Power of Expectancy	5
The Power To Succeed	8
The Power of Now	10
Unstoppable Power of Focus	12
The Power of Humanity	14
Cracks and Flaws	17
Give Yourself Permission To Live	19
The Power of Yes	21
The Power of You	24
Think...The 6 B's	26
Evidence of Confidence	28
The Power of Intention	31
Make the Impossible Possible	33
Make A Choice, Take A Chance, Create Change	36
The Way To Move Forward Is To Move Forward	38
The Power of A Seed	41
Take The Limits Off	43
Understanding Your Landscape	45
About Ryan/Testimonials	48-55

~ACKNOWLEDGMENTS~

Thank you to these people who empower and encourage me to expand and elevate my life forward, onward and upward:

Brooke Barefield
Viviane Brazil (iamhelping.com)
Melody Curry
Terrence Evans
Ms. JJ Fox & Cornelius "Cool C" Woodyard (foxtrapradio.com)
Will Hill
Bryan A. Jones (joshua-generation.net)
Dave Jordan
Tommie Mabry (tommiemabrycom.ipower.com)
DiMera Melvin
Shayla "Phriday" Patterson
Clovis Prince
Bobby Reed
Jason Thomas
Carlos Torres
James Walker
Owen & Martha Wallace (visionradio105.com)
Trell "Donk" Webb
April W. Welch

Lastly (but never least), this project would not be possible without these Educators doing the editing:

Tonya Collins
Marilyn Fuller
Kim Millen
Andrea Pritchett
DeShanta Reese

Pamela Sirmons
Sharil Smith
Jillian Wells
Kassia Walker

~FOREWORD~

I am truly privileged to have been "told" to write the Foreword to Ryan L. Jones' book *A Season of Change*. While only being invited to join a former friend to church to hear their 6'9", good-looking assistant pastor preach, never in a million years would I have thought that 20 years later, I would still be hearing this 6'9", good-looking minister preach. Twenty years ago, and until the present, Ryan still amazes me every time with his words, both spoken and written. Whether he is in the pulpit, in a classroom with students, in an auditorium full of professionals, on a street corner with the homeless, on one of his radio shows, delivering his quotes on social media, or even his thoughts in one of his books, Ryan communicates with passion – he speaks from his heart! Not only is he an ordained minister who teaches and preaches the Gospel, but he continues to dedicate his life to empowering people everywhere.

In reading the pages of this book, *A Season of Change*, I am absolutely astonished at Ryan's talents as not only a writer and published author, but also amazed at how these words are "motivating" and "transforming" to all who reads them. This book is unlike his last book, *Powerful Beyond Measure*, which is a book that consists of 50 quotes. Whereas, *A Season of Change* is a book that contains 20 short chapters that are intended to enlighten you to think deeper within yourselves to discover how and why you are the way you are, and that you do need change, (like the four seasons change) just as God would have us to do. As in nature, the seasons of this Earth presents many changes. Therefore, we as humans should realize that our lives also undergo seasons of change. In other words, just as seasons are not intended to be stagnant, neither are we. There are people and life's experiences that come and go, as well as in and out of our lives – those too are seasons of change. Moreover, in order for change to happen, often times, we may have to step out of our comfort zone, and be flexible for those changes to take place. One of the many lines that Ryan often says that I like when it comes to change is, "If you can't change the people around you; change the people around you." Those same people may bring about negative, as well as positive changes in and for your life. Ultimately, you need to recognize the seasons of change in your life and "PUSH" – **P**ray **U**ntil **S**omething (change) **H**appens!

Furthermore, reminiscent of what Ryan discusses in one of his chapters, we need to "take the limits off" and give ourselves "permission to take our lives to the next level". Determine and understand your landscape because we are all one-of-a-kind, created by God, and for a specific purpose. Thus, as stated in one of my favorite scriptures, Psalm 139:14, "I will give thanks and praise to you, for I am fearfully and wonderfully made; wonderful are your works, and my soul knows it very well."

To each and every one of you, read this, enjoy this, share this, and learn from this! The valuable applications throughout this book may change your life, as well as the lives of others that surround you. Finally, thank you again husband for wanting me to write the Foreword for this book A *Season of Change*. I already see some "seasonal changes" that I am going to make in my life, and others that I would consider for our family.

Karen R. Newman Jones, M.Ed., Ed.S.
Wife, Mother, Educator, Jones Family Manager
Dallas, Georgia
July, 2017

~INTRODUCTION~

"Now unto God who is able to do exceeding abundantly above all that I could ask or think."
Ephesians 3:20

When I wake up each day, my goal is to always and in all ways being open to becoming a life-long learner. Each day when I open my eyes, I ask the same question: *"How can I be of service today?"* Then I make the same statement: *"Great things are going to happen to me, through me and for me today!"* Lastly, I say my daily affirmation: *"I am Intentionally walking in Abundance, Excess, Increase and Overflow. This is MY season of Elevation and Expansion for which I am Humbled and Honored."*

God has truly blessed me to be able to speak life into so many people's life. I am grateful for all of the divine connections that I have been allowed to experience.

Because of so many people, but yet so few people, I have been given the task to make a global impact using my T.A.G.S...Talents, Abilities, Gifts and Skills. Many people have allowed me to speak life into their lives and a few people have spoken life into my life.

When I tell you, God has a way of bringing you into your "Season of Change." Growing up in a single parent household, the statistics stated that I would not make it this far in life. I had a 2.5 grade point average in high school and on the basketball court, I had a 1-point/1-rebound average. College was not supposed to happen. Thanks to Coach Willie Hill (from Morehouse College) who was walking through the gym on the way to the football field, stopped to watch us practice and asked Coach Arthur McAfee if he could recruit me to attend Morehouse. My best game at Morehouse College was against Alabama A&M College which was coached by Ben Jobe. NBA Hall of Famer, Alex English, told me to introduce myself to Coach Jobe. Let me tell you, God! When I wanted to leave Morehouse (my academics struggled), I was home for a break and told my high school Coach that I wanted to leave Morehouse, he said he had a friend at Southern University and he would call. A few days later, I got a call from the coach at Southern University and it was Ben Jobe. He was the new coach at Southern, and remembered my game against his old team. Two days later, I was on a plane to Baton Rouge.

When I graduated from Southern in 1993, I started to learn a little more about my "Cracks and Flaws" as well as working to "Make the Impossible Possible."

I got called into the ministry in 1990 and pastored my first church in 1998. When Karen and I got married in 1999, I was a mess (but I did not know it). She loved me through my mess (and still does). Because of what she has given me in my challenges, cracks, flaws, difficulties, shortcomings and struggles, I had to learn "self-care" and become all that this book talks about.

I am still a work in progress, but I am grateful for the process. As you read this book, I encourage you to "Take the Limits Off," "Give Yourself Permission to Live" and begin to live it "Bigger, Better, Brighter, Bolder, Braver and Badass."

Ryan J.

~A SEASON OF CHANGE~

Are you tired of doing the same thing the same way? Do you have faith, a greater level of expectancy and/or a vision? God wants to do something new in your life – today! God did not say maybe next week, next month or next year, but now.

No matter what you have gone through in the past, no matter how many setbacks you have suffered, no matter who or what has tried to frustrate your progress, today is a new day, and God will create a new, a now and a next thing in your life. Do not let your past determine your future!

If, you have been doing the same thing for your entire life and now want to go in a different direction, it is your choice. You have the power to do anything you want to do if you are willing to take responsibility for that power, and use it to achieve your heart's desire(s). It is important to try new things and embark upon a season of change in order to have a quality of life.

The Bible says, there is a season for everything in life (Ecclesiastes 3). If only we could embrace the seasons of our lives as willingly as we embrace the seasons of the year. It has been said that the only thing that is constant is change; unfortunately, that is what we tend to resist—especially if it means going outside our comfort zone.

The word 'season' usually refers to a period of time. When we think of seasons, we typically think of winter, spring, summer and fall. However, 'season' can also mean a time during which a certain activity is done…e.g. planting, fertilizing, pruning, harvesting, or storing. To this end, we must also recognize that at the beginning of each season, there is some sort of transition.

This is a time to let go of the old things and bring in the new. It may even be a time to show the people who are not supporting and loving you the door. This way, you can make room for positive and encouraging people to come in. It is time to get your hopes up; enlarge your vision and get ready for the new thing God has on the horizon. The Bible says, *"Behold, the former things are come to pass, and new things do I declare..."* (Isaiah 42:9) *"Behold, I will do a new thing..."* (Isaiah 43:19)

God has planned the seasons of your lives with infinite wisdom. God has ordained each season, knowing exactly what fruit is to be harvested during each time frame. I believe that since God's desire is to do us only good, God enjoys each season God plans for us (see Jer. 29:11). So why are we so prone to resist the season we are in?

Stepping into that new thing God has for us is not always easy. For some, walking out of and away from the old and into the new can be uncomfortable, stressful or downright scary. For others, we embrace changes in life as easily as we embrace the change of seasons.

Say good-bye to the last season. In order to fully embrace what is new, mark your passage from one season into the next. Embrace, enjoy and evolve in this new season. Once you have said good-bye, to the old, say "Hello" to what is New, Now and Next. THIS IS YOUR SEASON.

Believe, become and behold the changing of your season and know that God has ordained it to be so! Be an Innovator and Inventor of a new courage, now chance and next choice in your natural, normal and nourishing season.

God has amazing plans for your life! God wants you to fulfill your dreams and live a life of blessing, hope and promise. You will get there – as long as you are willing to do your part and trust God to do God's part. The more you lean on and trust in God through that process, the sooner you will be ready for whatever God has prepared for you.

~THE POWER OF "I AM"~

Throughout life you have been through a conditioning process that has created a mind-set overflowing with *"I AM" nots.*

"I AM". Two very powerful words. Two words that leave no room for doubt or fear. Two words that have the power to create or change your life. Whatever you say after those two words can and often does become your reality. As you describe yourself, so you define yourself. That is the power of "I AM" operating within you. You can now clearly appreciate how your "I AM" creates your reality.

The truth is it not the words themselves that have the power. It is the powerful spiritual beings that are using the words. Your words have to be repeated with attention, conviction and intention.

The words "I AM" which you consistently use to define who you are and what you are capable of, are holy expressions for the name of God—the highest aspect of yourself. To begin cultivating different results, it is necessary to change the action, beliefs, thoughts and words that serve as "the seed" and have created those conditions.

When you talk about yourself using "I AM" statements, you are essentially telling your whole being that you have decided that you are this, that or the other. It is a powerful message that is driven straight to and from your innermost being.

"I AM" is your true being. That is who you are. Additionally, whatever you attach to "I AM" with conviction, that is what you are and what you experience. This certainly makes a good case for being mindful when using the words, "I AM" to always follow them with some kind of idea.

Your "I AM" is a statement of being that transcends all dimensions. It can be felt and experienced as a unique sense of connection with your Life. When you affirm your "I AM" statements daily, your soul becomes totally identified with the truth of that statement at the very depths of consciousness where all human perceptions cease to influence the outcome and where all creation originates.

Romans 4 says to *"call the things that are not as though they were."* That simply means that you should not talk about the way you are. Rather, talk about the way you want to be. Your "I AM" should always be in the present tense...even if it has not yet manifested.

"I AM" is your true being. It is your real nature, yourself without any influences. It is your real identity, the Presence of God and All Living Power within us. That is who you are, and whatever you attach to "I AM" with conviction, that is what you are and what you experience.

"I AM" is a powerful declaration. Whatever comes after "I AM"..." is a declaration of what, who and how you are. "I AM" is your Perspective. "I AM" is your

Present and Presence. "I AM" is Personal. "I AM" is your Purpose.

Creating your positive "I AM" statements is a very easy process. On a piece of paper or on your computer make a list of "I AM" statements that you believe to be true about yourself. Keep going until you cannot think of any more. These can be anything that you really believe about yourself. Recognize that these are layers of the ego that have been programmed into your subconscious and that you have the power to change them! Pick a few, then stand in front of a mirror, look yourself in the eye and say "I AM _____."

Write it down. Look at yourself again, and say "I AM _____." Write it down. Repeat this process for at least 15 minutes. Set the list aside for 24 hours. Then pick it up again and review your list. If there is anything negative or limiting at all, cross it out. Make sure it is completely blacked out so that you cannot read it anymore.

~THE POWER OF EXPECTANCY~

Expectancy is: the state of expecting that something, especially something good, will happen. In other words, expectancy is the force that attracts things to you. Your level of expectancy is greater than you know. In order to raise your level of expectancy, you have to change your focus. You have to change what you desire in your life. You have to believe and have faith that you will go to new levels of victory and expectancy. You set the standard on what you accomplish and how high you will go in life. Anyone who truly wants to experience life at his or her potential must practice the principle of expectancy: persistence, prepare and preserve.

Expectancy is a powerful magnet, perhaps as powerful as desire. Once you believe you can get what you want, it becomes possible to expect it and expect it bigger, better, brighter, braver and bolder to be manifested.

The one ingredient that turns the ordinary to extraordinary is merely a commitment to excellence. Excellence in our personal and professional development simply requires that you constantly produce results beyond the ordinary and always going beyond your limits. It will change your results to that of having the quality of life in which you thrive and grow, rather than believing that an average or mediocre result is acceptable.

What you keep before your eyes will affect you. You will produce what you are continually seeing in your mind. If you dwell on positive thoughts, your life will move in that direction. If you continually think negative thoughts, you will live a negative life. That is why you need to raise your level of expectancy. You have to change your thinking before you can change your life. "Set your mind on things above." If you will change your thinking, you will change your life.

Do not become so caught up in a small matter that you cannot take advantage of important opportunities. Most people spend their entire lives letting down buckets into empty wells and then waste their days trying to pull them up again. Expect more than others think possible; dream more than others think is practical; risk more than others think is safe. EXPECT! Remember, in the eyes and sight of average people, average is always considered outstanding.

Your expectancy will shift to that of "expect and see" rather than "expecting to fail."

Where attention goes, energy flows. Where intention goes, energy flows.

This means that wherever you put your expectancy, or your attention, is what you will create and experience. It is very powerful to 'act as if' and just proceed in life expecting something to work out the way you desire, whether or not you have physical proof that it seems likely or possible.

Expectancy is a powerful magnet, perhaps as powerful as desire. Those who get ahead in life have positive expectations for themselves. They believe in their ability to figure things out no matter what happens or what opportunity they chase after in life. They understand that there will be struggle along their path but they choose to stay resilient and continue taking steps forward.

Like attracts like, so expect good things to come to you all the time in expected and unexpected ways. Expect it to be so! Whatever we vividly imagine, ardently desire, sincerely believe, and enthusiastically act upon must inevitably come upon to pass.

The Power of Expectancy is more than simple hope, optimism or wishing things will work out the way you want. Expectation is a source of excitement that empowers you, elevates you and expand you.

With all of that, expect what you want and want what you expect.

~THE POWER TO SUCCEED~

What is the difference between successful people and unsuccessful people? It is as simple as this: successful people talk and think about what they are creating while unsuccessful people focus on and talk about what they are lacking and do not have.

So how do you bridge that gap between wanting success and having your success? Let us make an important distinction. There is a big difference between "Wanting" something and "Having" something.

Wanting means the absence of something or lacking something. Deficient in some aspect, part or thing.

Having means to get, to experience, to hold, to possess, to receive.

You can have one or the other, but not both at the same time with any particular object of your desire. You either have it or you do not. Successful people have tapped into the hidden power of their subconscious mind and they know how to work with and apply mind power to get what they want.

Believe it or not, the most important quality required to succeed in life is belief. The Power to Succeed is a series of choices that you make based on what you believe is possible for yourself – that results in an outcome. It is not luck and is not something you learn at school – not really. It comes from life experience.

Along with that, the most important belief is self-belief. You may not think it is significant, but you have the power in you to achieve success and you also have the ability to fail by not trying and not believing in yourself.

Now you may not do this consciously, but you do engage your subconscious mind and get this power to work for you regularly.

You were born with the potential and promises to walk an extraordinary significant and successful path. God gave you the courage and confidence to succeed. As a matter of fact, God wants all of us to succeed. Proverbs 16:3 says, *"Commit your actions to the LORD, and your plans will succeed."* So, you do not have the right to turn into a backward coward before moving forward, onward and upward as God has planned. Doing the best at this moment puts you in the best and blessed place for the next. Come what may, you must stand firm to the thoughts that you will not be beaten but will succeed because God said so.

Visualize yourself getting what you want and succeeding. Always believe that you can and will succeed. Mind power relies on your thoughts, beliefs and how you see yourself. Make them all positive and your subconscious mind will deliver.

Be consistent and be persistent - You have to focus on your goals, have positive thoughts and positive beliefs every day. It is true that success takes time to build and maybe getting a head start is just what you need. And wherever you are, right now, is your starting point. It also requires that you experiment, try things and not fear tripping up or even falling on your face every now and then. It is critical to know that every big success is built on lots of little failures. Because without them – how do you learn what does not work?

May you never bow to failure, and when you are faced with a challenge or setback, see it as only an experience for a rematch. Know that fear is a lack of faith and vision and you must have the courage to succeed.

Many people overestimate what they can do in a year and underestimate what they can do in a lifetime. Remember, your highest potential is not to be confused with your highest performance level.

You have the Power to Succeed and make great, greater and the greatest things happen to you, through you and for you.

~THE POWER OF NOW~

Today, like every day, is yours for you to live your life now! Much of your past, just like history, has a way of repeating itself. The more you look backwards, the less you are able to look and move forward, onward and upward. Be PRESENT and in the NOW!

To a large degree, the measure of your peace of mind is determined by how you are able to live in the present moment. The best thing about it is that it comes upon you one day at a time.

Whatever it holds, live now because today is yours! If you worry about what might be and wonder what might have been you will miss what is. Live now because the day belongs to you if you make the adjustments, have a positive attitude and take authority to make it happen.

If you have tried to live in the present moment, you know how hard it is. "Be present" is one of those phrases -- just like "be positive" that sounds easy but is really quite difficult to put into practice. If you are struggling with staying present in your life, know that you are not alone. It is a very tough thing to do, so much so, that I have to wonder if even those who are experts on the matter are really able to stay present all the time. It is so easy to write the words "stay in the now moment" and really mean them as true and honest advice, but it is so much more difficult to actually stay in the now moment with thoughts being as they are.

One of the hardest things to do in this constantly moving world is to actually live in the moment. While in a moment, you must choose to live in it — good or bad — and take something away from every experience to ensure you have a better tomorrow, no matter how small, or slight, that moment may seem. At the end of the moment, no matter how much you wish, hope and pray, the past is the past and the future is ahead.

If you are living in the present, you are living in acceptance. You are accepting life as it is now, not as how you wish it would have been. If you are delaying your happiness and your joy for "one day" you are living on the horizon, rather than living in the here and now. Horizon living will leave you feeling like you are always chasing a carrot that you never quite get.

Face it, the only thing that exists is what is happening right now. The past does not exist – it is over with and should be nothing but a fading memory. The future does not exist - it simply has not happened yet. Both the past and the future are merely concepts which consist of thoughts and memories. The only thing that really exists right now is the very present moment that you live in and from this present moment you can draw tremendous power - the kind of power that can change your life and allow you to achieve your goals.

Do not ignore living in the now because the present moment is all you have. From this day forward, you must choose to live in the now and navigate your life moment by moment.

If we really do want to be present in the here-and-now, we ultimately have to achieve some level of happiness, enough to satisfy that seemingly insatiable drive within us to continue wanting more and more.

The good life is "out there" beyond the present moment, close enough for you to see it, but not close enough for it to be yours. If you keep living on the horizon, you will never really step into happiness, live your purpose, or get the most out of life. To end horizon living and live your best live now. Life is happening in the present moment. Step into it today. Create the life you want NOW.

All it takes to live your life to the fullest is courage- nothing more, nothing less. This sounds rather minimalist and easy to cope with, but a lack of courage is a key factor that prevents most people from living their lives to the fullest. Be the one to stand out in the crowd.

~THE UNSTOPPABLE POWER OF FOCUS~

God is constantly trying to plant new seeds of victory inside of you by increasing you and enlarging your vision. God wants to take you to new levels in victory. But in order for this to happen, the seed has to take root in your heart. If you are ever going to be successful, you have to see yourself as such. Before your dreams come to pass, you have to look through your eyes of faith and see them come to pass.

Learning to focus on one thing is possibly one of the best things you can do to invest in yourself. This is probably one of the most overlooked areas of self-improvement.

There will be those who do not want you to fulfill your destiny, so they will try to discourage you and uproot the seed God planted. In order to defeat the "haters" in your life, you have to stay focused on your future.

If you continue to stay focused, you will begin to see the Plans and Purpose of God placed in your heart come to pass-dreams filled with blessings and victory! Do not waste your tomorrows wondering on your yesterdays. You need to reach for the potential and not be restricted by the past. The past is past; it has no life. Know where you are coming from and you will know where to go. Know where to go and you will be there.

If you focus too much on the past, you will be held back by limitations that may no longer even exist. Instead, look forward with positive expectation, and you will find yourself quickly moving in a Forward, Onward and Upward direction.

The more you look backward, the less you are able to look forward. Remember, Jesus said in Luke 9:62, *"No man, having put his hand to the plough, and looking back, is fit for the kingdom of God."*

If you focus only on what you do not have, you are likely to perpetuate the same circumstances for yourself. True happiness is a state of mind, not a collection of material goods or a set number of goals achieved.

If you look on what you already have with gratitude and give thanks and bless it for being in your life, you will reprogram your brain to notice all of the good things in life. You must take care to pay full attention to what you are feeling, hearing, seeing, smelling and tasting.

Pretty straight forward and good advice, right? Well, I thought so until I saw another angle regarding focus. It is great to follow the above steps on how to get focused, but the way you remain focused is by being unflappable, motivated, persistent and able to continue to persevere even in times of uncertainty. If you are clear–and I mean absolutely clear on what your focus is, then you need to continue your FOCUS, in other words Follow One's Course Until Successful.

It is so easy to get distracted and lose focus. But, when you are unflappable, you are staying in control of your focus. When you are motivated, you are self-energized and able to maintain your focus even when others around you are not.

When you are persistent, you are relentless in your focus and refuse to become distracted. When you persevere, you stay the course; you do not waiver and you keep your eye on your goal. Staying focused is not always easy, but it is possible. Learn what steps are needed for you to stay FOCUSED and then Follow One's Course Until Successful!

I challenge you to FOCUS on these things (and more): what you are Pursuing; Your Plan; Your Purpose; Your Possibilities; Your Potential; Your Promises; Your Passion; Your Power to Prosper and Your Positive Position.

~THE POWER OF HUMILITY~

People often confuse humility with weakness. Humility carries the same weight as water. It provides the power you need in life to sustain. Humility is an abstract form but holds an essence of life. In order to experience its power, you have to merge with it and you have to allow it to show you the way back to yourself, back to the Light and back to Life. Do not underestimate the power of humility.

The acceptance of humility allows you to see and appreciate yourself in a different way. Your ability to accept your imperfections takes your ego down to see that the world will go on no matter how great you are. The power that unleashes due to recognition of humility gains incredible power. The power you gain by being humble is that of being respected by others. When you are arrogant, it will turn people off. But if you are humble, you will be able to attract the masses into your life.

Humility is the act of being modest, reverential even politely submissive. It is the opposite of aggression, arrogance, pride and vanity. Humility offers its owner complete freedom from the desire to impress, be right, or get ahead. Frustrations and losses have less impact on a humble ego and a humble person confidently receives opportunity to grow, improve, and reject society's labels. A humble life results in compassion, contentment, forgiveness and patience.

Humility is a choice that listens more and speaks less. C. S. Lewis said, *"True humility is not thinking less of yourself; it is thinking of yourself less."*

Something empowering about humility is the effect that it has on others who notice the difference. The road to humility is a continuous cycle that never exhausts if your attention is on the goal and understanding what is important.

Humility understands individual limitations. Humble people realize weakness and embrace it. As a result, they wisely look for answers outside of themselves. A humble person appreciates the fact that the world does not revolve around him or her. And accepts their position as just a tiny piece in the giant puzzle.

Humility respects others and their opinions. An opinion is meant to be different and should not be seen as a wrong statement. I am only saying that it is not wrong just because it is different... and that is a far better place to begin the dialogue. Humility listens more and speaks less. It spends more time understanding... and less time being understood.

Humility withholds judgments over intentions as much as possible. The quickest way to win an argument in your mind is to make sweeping judgements concerning the intentions of others. Humility helps others and promotes others. Joy is not found in being right and arriving at the top. Instead, joy is found in helping others grow and succeed. Humility realizes that in those cases, both win.

Humility always begins in our heart. As a result, it offers significant control over action, attitude and outlook. It has nothing to prove, but everything to offer.

Humility always begins in our heart. As a result, it offers significant control over actions, attitude and outlook. It has nothing to prove, but everything to offer.

Great leaders are humble enough to get out of their own way, and lead others to greatness. Humble people are able to encourage others and accept their talents, their abilities, their gifts and their skills....working together for their good. Humility is what gives you power. Your humility is not pride!

~CRACKS AND FLAWS~

An elderly Chinese woman had two large pots, each hung on the ends of a pole which she carried across her neck. One of the pots had a crack in it while the other pot was perfect and always delivered a full portion of water. At the end of the long walks from the stream to the house, the cracked pot arrived only half full. For a full two years this went on daily, with the woman bringing home only one and a half pots of water. Of course, the perfect pot was proud of its accomplishments. But the poor cracked pot was ashamed of its own imperfection, and miserable that it could only do half of what it had been made to do.

After two years of what it perceived to be bitter failure, it spoke to the woman one day by the stream. 'I am ashamed of myself, because this crack in my side causes water to leak out all the way back to your house.' The old woman smiled, 'Did you notice that there are flowers on your side of the path, but not on the other pot's side?' 'That's because I have always known about your flaw, so I planted flower seeds on your side of the path, and every day while we walk back, you water them.' For two years I have been able to pick these beautiful flowers to decorate the table. Without you being just the way you are, there would not be this beauty to grace the house.' Each of us has our own unique flaw. But it's the cracks and flaws we each have that make our lives together so very interesting and rewarding. You've just got to take each person for what they are and look for the good in them."

It is human nature to focus on the negative aspects about ourselves, yet it is also very harmful to our emotional, mental and physical well-being. Having imperfections is what uniqueness is all about. It is not about what others think, it is about what you think of yourself. If you are ashamed of this, how will you be able to be you best self? Stop focusing on your flaws and begin embracing them.

All of us have cracks and flaws and we wear them like scars, trying to hide behind them, covering them or masking them. We live our lives working out ways to hide them from the outside world, without ever really letting them see light. Whatever else you want to call 'the perfect this' or 'the perfect that,' there will be a million people who disagree with your definition, and vice versa.

Evaluate your emotional baggage, personality traits and the physical things around you. Do you think your personality traits will be imperfect or perfect? Forget about what you think anyone else may think about these things. You will never know for sure anyway. Plus, it does not matter what anyone else thinks. It matters what you think, how you feel about yourself. Then find a way to accept, embrace and ultimately love each and every one of those pieces of baggage, things and traits.

Your cracks and flaws are who you are, and the more you hide them away, the more you hide yourself against the world. Your imperfections are what makes you the individual you are. The sooner you start realizing that your flaws are what make you beautiful, the sooner we can stop calling them flaws.

Remember that your imperfections turns out to be perfections and are blessings in disguise. Your cracks, flaws and imperfections, as you see them, are different in God's eyes. We are all different, and we all have a purpose. Embrace your cracks and flaws knowing that God has made you who you are for a reason.

So, the true moral of your story: each of us have our own unique cracks and flaws. We are all cracked pots. But it is the cracks and flaws we each have that makes our lives together so rewarding. We have to take each person for what they are, and look for the good in them.

You were born an original, do not die a copy. Be cracked. Be flawed. Be perfectly imperfect. Be you. Just be.

~GIVE YOURSELF PERMISSION TO LIVE~

When was the last time you gave yourself permission to do something you really wanted to do for yourself? Give full permission to be yourself to be, do and to have the things you really want.

Permission is a very powerful word. It is a word that can enslave you to your own doubts and fears or set you free to pursue your dreams. It gives you some living room...a lot of 'living' room.

You are so resilient and so much stronger than you think. Celebrate yourself and create a major shift so you can make this world a better place. Every morning, ask life to show you how you can help create more compassion, gentleness, love, kindness and peace.

Give yourself permission for everything. Permission to make Mistakes. Permission to be Alive. Permission to Achieve. Permission to have Abundance. Permission to Accept (instead of correct or dismiss) praise. Permission to have Accomplishments. Permission to get Angry. Permission to React...to cry, to laugh, to scream. Permission to have an Attitude. Permission to be Amazing. Permission to Anticipate. Permission to Appreciate. Permission to set your Atmosphere. Permission to pay Attention to dreams, goals and vision. Permission to be Authentic and take Authority. Permission to be Awesome.

The only person that truly needs to live with your life decisions every day is you. When you start listening to your own voice and taking steps that make you happy your life starts to change. It is not necessarily a rapid transformation but it is a real one where every decision you make guided by your own feelings gets you closer to living your best life.

If you are living a life bound by other people's expectations I challenge you to start taking control by giving yourself permission to do great things that light you up. You might be surprised at where it takes you.

Give yourself permission to remove toxic people from your life. Give yourself permission to say "yes" to what you want. Give yourself permission to live your life by design and not by default. Give yourself permission to go, grow and glow. This is your life, live it in full and glorious color.

Remind yourself that you are an Authentic, Custom-Made, One-Of-A-Kind, Original, Unique individual, and what is truly important to you, is what is "right." Practice being self-centered – not in an egotistical way, but in a way that serves your life best. Only from a place of "centeredness" can you make the best decisions for yourself, reach your goals, and be of greatest service to others. It is time for you stand closer to the center of your own being, and stop betraying yourself to please others. In other words, Stop Asking Permission To Live Your Best Life.

Permission comes from *within* you, and you are 100% responsible for granting it. It is completely within your power because there is only one person that needs to give you permission to live a life of greatness: YOU! Until you fully allow yourself to live the life you want, you will find it impossible to live up to your greatest potential.

Granting yourself permission to be who you are right now, and acknowledge who you want to be. It does not require you to give up something, it encourages you to give something positive to yourself.

Giving yourself permission allows you to shift your mindset from what you think you should do, to choosing what is right for you. Giving yourself permission to be you nurtures positive choices and greater happiness.

Whatever it is you feel you need permission for, go ahead and grant that permission to yourself now!

~THE POWER OF YES~

Two of the most powerful and empowering words in the universe are "Yes" and "No." Meaning them is key to identifying your integrity. You have the amazing ability to bring into existence, precisely that which you declare with your words. When you say yes to something, you are actually saying, "so it is said, let it be done." You are creating your world, by the words you speak out loud.

Each and every "Yes" you say when you mean it is a true "Yes." Each "Yes" muttered with an unintentional heart is a false "yes." A true "Yes" is a wholehearted commitment and consciousness of attention and energy to whatever you have said "Yes" to. You can only give a true "Yes" to something that is true for you. What is true for you is always life giving and increases your aliveness.

A true "Yes" sparks your full engagement. It focuses your energy and attention, enlivens and energizes you and calls forth an expanded or deeper expression of your authentic self. A true "yes" or "no" is essentially a Yes! The "Yes" is to you, your truth and the Spirit within. And to the truth and the Spirit within everyone involved. Ultimately, you are saying "Yes" to Life. Each time you say "Yes" to Life, Life resoundingly says an even bigger "Yes" to you.

When you use the power of "Yes" and Say *"Yes" to yourself,* the universe "hears" that you have the intention to make yourself a priority. And when you communicate to the universe that you are willing to put yourself first, the universe will help you by delivering the "here" you want more of in your life!

Saying "Yes" to YOU is the foundation for taking a stand for yourself. Each time you say "Yes" to you is an act of valuing yourself. Saying "Yes" to you is ultimately about aliveness. Your "Yes" is a powerful manifestation tool. On a deeper level it is a powerful doorway into our personal awakening. By saying "Yes," you claim your own personal power and birth right to remember and live as an awakening living being. So, say "Yes." In fact, say "Yes" as often as you can. What you put in motion stays in motion. What you put to rest, stays at rest.

Saying "Yes" means making the most of every opportunity and encounter. It means taking chances to stretch your comfort zone, to overcome your insecurities, to beat your fear, to get through criticism, embarrassment failure and rejection with a positive spirit. It essentially means knowing what you need "more of" in your life to help you live a more optimal life. And often the things you most you resist because they make you feel uncomfortable.

"Yes" is a tiny word that can do big things and it needs to be said often. Saying "Yes" requires accountability, commitment and work. It can sometimes scares people away, especially if you feel unmotivated and unprepared. But here is your reality: a "Yes" will always give you more in life than a "No." Your "Yes" will do things in your life that you have never expected. You will see things being manifested for your greater good by using and understanding the power of YOUR "Yes." Make sure that your "Yes" is a significant "Yes."

When you say "Yes" to something, you are automatically saying no to something else. The response "Yes, and" can unlock the true power of saying "Yes." When you say "Yes," you are opening the door on opportunity; an opportunity to learn, an opportunity to grow and an opportunity to blow your own mind. So say "Yes," and watch the doors swing wide open.

So what is the big deal, right? Saying "Yes" in all areas of your life possibly would not make much of a difference as to how you live your life. And "Yes," that can certainly be true. It might not make much of a difference at all, but on the other hand, it just might.

One of the most effective means for transcending the ordinary and moving into the realm of extraordinary is saying "Yes" more frequently and eliminating no almost completely. Make a list of things that you should be saying "YES" to that will help you live a more optimal life. Step Into Your Greatness! Say "Yes" to you and feel fully alive!

~THE POWER OF YOU~

It is time to connect with the power of YOU! Let these clichés sink in for a moment: You are the bomb dot com. You are awesome. You are better than good, better than most and sometimes better than that! You are the shit.

If you do not believe me, the shame is on you! But I understand your skepticism – there is a whole world out there trying to convince you otherwise, as if you are not "all of that and a bag of chips!"

You! What is in you is the answer to your problems. You can seek outside help; but there is no outside solution. The solution has to come from within. It is more important to become and be than it is to get and possess. What you carry inside of yourself will take you further than what carries you. Your outlook determines your outcome. What you think about, you bring about.

You are an Authentic, Custom-Made, One-Of-A-Kind, Original, Unique You! In this world of billions of people there is no one exactly like you and that makes you unique. You owe it to the world to share your uniqueness with those around you. The world should not have to miss out on your beauty, blessings, brilliance and a bit of badassness!

We all have a different life journey and a different story to tell; we all face different challenges and gain different experiences. There are billions of people on this planet, yet YOU are the only person who is exactly like you.

No matter who you are, you can provide value. You have an individual purpose that cannot be compared to everyone else. You have a different perspective to share. You can shed light on a situation that maybe no one else can possibly provide. You can utilize your unique experiences to help and positively influence others.

At the end of the day, always remember that you are important and you cannot, do not and must not compare yourself to anyone else. You have all of your unique T.A.G.S...Talents, Abilities, Gifts and Skills. Always remain grateful and gracious; compassionate and passionate, and also, always believe that your ordinary will become extraordinary.

In other words, learn the power within you. This is not so much about religion or spirituality, although faith in a higher power helps to ground us. This is about how your past and the feelings generated from painful situations have affected you.

You and your thoughts are very powerful. What you think shapes not only who you are but also what happens to you. Your thoughts create the feelings within you that create the actions you do. Thus the results you get are based upon your actions, whether intended or not.

You may need to change your thoughts. You may even need to change how you think. This means that you have to be totally honest with yourself. Your thoughts could be blocking you from being the person that you want to and should be.

Before you can achieve any level of success, you must first change how you think about yourself. This starts with courage; having the courage to acknowledge how you feel about yourself; having the courage to understand why you feel the way you do.

The power of you is indeed in you. Allow your thoughts to manifest the power of you!

As Gandhi says, "Be the change you want to see in the world".

~THINK BIGGER, BETTER, BRAVER, BRIGHTER, BOLDER & BADASS~

Think Bigger, Better, Braver, Brighter, and Bolder with a little bit of Badass. "The only difference between ordinary and extraordinary is a lot of extra." Most people desire to feel better, do better, know better and be better.

You are capable of raising yourself to new levels in life. I believe that in order for you to live the Bigger, Better, Braver, Brighter and Bolder Extraordinary Life that you are meant to live, it is going to take Dedication, Expectation, Inspiration, Liberation, Motivation, Perspiration and Transformation.

Being Bigger, Better, Braver, Brighter, Bolder and Badass means that you are not that person today than you were yesterday, last week, last month or even last year. You have learned valuable life lessons from your experiences and now use them to make you a Bigger, Better, Braver, Brighter, Bolder and a little bit of a Badass person.

Do not get caught up with your perceived limitations. Think big and work hard to attain those dreams and desires that you want in life. As you step up the ladder of progress, you will just about find out that

Your impossible has just become a little bit more possible.

You can achieve as much as you would like. It is all a matter of how bold you are willing to be. It is about how big you want to play. Some people do not like to aim high in case they fail and do not achieve them. To save face, you might focus on all the things that could go wrong and avoid dreaming of all the things that can go right. Like spinning wheels on a car that is stuck in the mud, this holds you back and keeps you exactly where you are. Whatever you dream is, why not make it Bigger, Better, Braver, Brighter, Bolder and Badass?

The more dreams you have and the bigger they are, the more you will achieve. Go for it. Be outrageous, think of everything that you would really want and go Bigger! Go Better! Go Braver! Go Brighter! Go Bolder! Go Badass!

Thinking big and aiming high breaks you out of making incremental improvements and causes you to think and work differently. It forces you to break away from what worked in the past and to explore new ways of working.

The only way you can achieve something big is to think big. Big ideas and big vision demands a significant shift in your capabilities. It stimulates innovation, new approaches and ways of conducting your business. It forces you out of your comfort zone without which you will fail to make progress.

In an effort to let in the Bigger, Better, Braver, Brighter, Bolder and Badass life you were meant to live allows you to be more excited about it, make the decision to start living life now that a new awareness is dawning upon you.

What you see going on around you and in your world is an invite from life urging you to dream Bigger, Better, Braver, Brighter, Bolder and Badass dreams for yourself so you can create way more than what others before you were able to.

You have a choice, and you are the only one who can control what your Bigger, Better, Braver, Brighter and Bolder with a little bit of Badass Extraordinary Life means. It means having the courage to be exactly who you are without apology. It means focusing on what is going on right now and that is *you*!

Do not just think big, think big about big things: who you are, why you are here, what you can contribute to the world, how life should be lived. Trivialize the trivial.

Strive only for what is worth striving for. And be sure to turn big thinking into big action. Exist significantly, expansively. Try to achieve something important that no one else has. What could you create that you would be proud to have as the only evidence that you had ever existed. Get started on creating it...Today!

~THE EVIDENCE OF CONFIDENCE~

Confidence. I define it as your belief in yourself; it is having assurance and self-reliance of your TAGS...Talents, Abilities, Gifts and Skills...regardless of the situation you are in. Finding a healthy balance can be challenging. Too much of it and you can come off as cocky and stumble into unforeseen obstacles, but having too little can prevent you from taking risks and seizing opportunities.

You did not come out of the womb and into the world unsure of your cry or insecure about your large umbilical cord. You came out and into this world unaware of external judgment, concerned only with your own experience and needs. By no means am I suggesting that you should be oblivious to other people. It is just that it may help to remember confidence was your original nature before time started taking it away from you.

Confidence comes down to one simple question: If you do not believe in yourself, how do you expect anybody else to? Self-confident people are admired by others and inspire confidence in others. They face their fears head-on and tend to be risk takers. They know that no matter what obstacles come their way, they have the ability to get past them. Self-confident people tend to see their lives in a positive light even when things are not going so well, and they are typically satisfied with and respect themselves.

Confidence is staying away from negativity and bringing on the positivity. When you take that weight off your shoulders and realize that sometimes the twists and turns have nothing to do with what you did or should have done, it is easier to feel confident in what you bring to the table.

I encourage you to believe that you can do things to increase your confidence. You do not have to rely or look to other to increase your confidence. And if you believe that you are competent and courageous, you can become someone worthy of respect, and someone who can pursue what you want despite what other people may say or think about you.

The key is to be true to yourself, to be true to the very best that is in you, and to live your life consistent with your highest values and aspirations. The evidence of confidence enables you to faithfully and fearlessly pursue your biggest desires and dreams. It equips you to conquer your challenges, no matter how big they may seem to me. It sets you off to live your greatest life possible.

If you believe you are capable, you will feel confident. If you believe in yourself, this simply means you believe that you are someone of positive value, and you also believe you are capable of achieving things you want to achieve, like your personal dreams, goals and hopes. As simple as it sounds, just by having these kinds of beliefs, you are naturally a more self-confident person, and therefore also happier and more successful.

Negative thinking, over thinking, and living in your head will absolutely kill you when it comes to confidence. Mind your own thoughts, stay positive and focused on your goals, ignore self-doubt and criticism, visualize and concentrate on what you want and you will eventually have it.

When you start feeling unsure of yourself remember: we were all born with the evidence of confidence, and you can all get it back if you learn to tune out the negative thoughts that threaten it. You can take control of your life, become the person everyone wants to know, and feel the surging power of confidence that shines with excitement (rather than fear) through you as you walk into the room.

Like anything else in life, your confidence will improve with practice and time (this is not an overnight phenomenon). Take small actions every day to improve your confidence and retrain your brain to learn positive new ways of thinking and believing. Challenge yourself to stretch beyond your comfort zone of confidence to prove to yourself what you are truly capable of achieving. With every incremental step forward, your confidence will grow exponentially.

~THE POWER OF INTENTION~

Your intentions create your reality. You do not attract what you want, you attract what you are. A day without intention is a day wasted. Bold words, but ones I firmly believe.

Intention: the thing that you plan to do or achieve: an aim or purpose — Merriam Webster

To create an intention is to clarify what you want to achieve: Clear intention is the most powerful creation we have available to us. Intention is about Attention.

When you decide on clear intentionality or choose to do a particular thing in our life and take an action or step towards that intention, the universe responds and actually begins to bring into our life the circumstances that will allow that thought to manifest within a way which can be supported by the environment in which you find yourselves.

Remember to also take a moment to put the power of thought and intention behind your action....think, consider, and then act. You will avoid regrets and produce positive, powerful and productive results. Think before you go and where you will end up is just where you intended to be.

Intention is the seed of every dream and it is your deepest intentions that ultimately shape your destiny.

Big picture stuff, I know. But think about it. An intention is a channeled impulse of consciousness. And it is only when you release your intentions (or impulses) into the universe that you allow them to truly grow and become real.

To put it another way: if your intentions are the seeds of your dreams, then releasing them into the universe is like planting these seeds into fertile ground. They need this to grow.

The way in which you release your intentions is important too. This must be done in a relaxed, positive and healthy manner. The true power of intention manifests only when it comes from a place of contentment and acceptance, not a place of scarcity or need. For this reason, you must release your intentions calmly and positively – and then detach from the outcome.

What needs to be understood is that we will not, and cannot, give our attention to something unless we have an intention. Your intention is the underlying purpose for where you are placing your attention.

Your intention may be only to see what it is that crossed our peripheral vision or caused the sound that we may have heard. But, nevertheless there is still an intention behind your attention. You may be only placing your attention on something out of curiosity, something that you desire for information about whatever it is that captured your attention, or it may be out of fear you may be harmed.

An intention can be seen from several different perspectives, all of which ultimately achieve the same end - it directs and underlies your attention. An intent is normally seen as a purpose, aim, goal or design. More importantly for our purposes, intent is the act of intending and is actually a state of mind in which, or the purpose with which, one does an act. Here the action you refer to is how, why and where you place your attention.

Let your intentions be very calculated, clear and conscious. When you begin to utilize the Power of Intention - you will begin to get dramatic results in your life.

The power of intention is the ability to clearly understand what you want, why you want it and how you plan on going about achieving that goal. You need to talk about "setting intentions" and "creating your reality."

When belief takes hold, manifesting is inevitable. So, if you are working towards a goal, remember that everything begins with a thought. Begin by clarifying what you desire and then put it out there; let the universe know what you want. Once this happens, believe that you deserve it. Always remember, if you believe it, you will achieve it.

By setting your intentions every day in a purposeful way, you become the director of your life because the Universe will always support your thoughts. Your power of intention is an internal force to be reckoned with, so be mindful of what intentions you are setting because when you make your intentions powerful, you have a powerful life.

~MAKE THE IMPOSSIBLE, POSSIBLE~

You have discovered something you are very passionate about and you tell your family and friends about your dream and idea. You are really excited to share your dream and idea for a new venture and you know that everyone will be just as excited as you are. Then you realize that they are not. The people closest to you tell you that you are crazy and the idea was just as crazy. They give you a million and one reasons why your idea is stupid and will never work.

Because they killed your dream and idea, you walk away defeated, deflated and maybe depressed. You tell yourself that they are right and that you should not have ever considered or thought about it.

You put your dream and idea, that passionate spark, back down inside you and go on with your less-than-passionate life. But you know the spark will not go away. If you do not find a way to express it – your talents, abilities, gifts and skills to the world – it will eat you from the inside and drive you crazy until you do something about it.

So, in order to make the impossible possible, you must believe that all things are possible for you. Believe that you can change your altitude, environment, levels, position and status. Begin by allowing yourself to believe that what you want is achievable, possible and reachable and that you deserve all of it.

Your beliefs in the possible and your possibilities are powerful. If you believe something is impossible, that belief will destroy your confidence and turn that impossible belief into a self-fulfilling prophecy. If a person with authority tells you that you "cannot" do something, you will believe it, even if that person's prediction is not accurate. And once you believe it, you will behave as if that prediction is true, by default making it come true.

Your positive beliefs are just as powerful. If you believe you can and will do something, you will find the means to make the impossible possible. Believing that something is possible is the first step towards fearlessly reaching goals.

Give yourself permission to believe and dream the impossible. Whatever experiences, people, places or pursuits you have until now been too afraid or ashamed or cautious to seek – start seeking them out today!

As you know, to create something in your reality you must be able to first create it in your mind's eye. So go ahead – spend some time living in your dreams. Imagine in detail what living out your wildest dreams feels, looks, smells, sound and tastes like.

Your life will not change until you take action and change it. Take imperfect action. Do not wait for the stars to align before doing anything. Do something – anything – today. Stop waiting for someone to give you permission. No one is holding you back but you.

If you have a passion to do or be something, you need to believe it is possible to achieve it. If you start off with the idea that it is impossible, you will quit at the first minor challenge. However, challenges will not stop you when you believe something is possible. Instead, you will look for ways to overcome any challenges knowing that there are ways that you can overcome them.

Making the impossible possible is about being true to your life's happiness and the higher calling within you. You never know – you may find a different, more brilliant dream on your way.

Your "impossible" dreams are possible. The only way to achieve the impossible is to believe it is possible.

~MAKE A CHOICE. TAKE A CHANCE. CREATE CHANGE~

It is all up to you. Winning the lottery does not compare to the potential that is dormant but is waiting on you to explore. It is sad that many people are more willing to try their luck in a gambling casino rather than take a chance on themselves. Three barriers that halt you from taking a chance and creating your winning opportunities are: Faithlessness, False facts and Fear. When you are down to your last dollar, count on hope and do not let indifference rob you from taking one more chance.

When you are BE-ing the kind of person that is most desirable for you to be, then you will automatically do the best you can do—then you will have the peace and whatever else that is most desirable in life for you to have.

Take a Chance, Be the Change and Make a Choice / (CHA)lle(NGE)d yourself to make this your REALity.

When you think of a successful person, what questions come to mine regarding how they got there? Did they succeed the first time or did they experience several failures before favorable outcomes? Regardless of the road traveled, the commonality is failure is likely to occur before success.

Expect some failures in your life. If you do not experience any failures, it is likely you have not taken any risks. Learn from failure and use it to motivate you to keep going until you get it right.

Chances. Changes. Choices. Three simple words that have the power to bring you where you want to be. Right here and now.

It is important to frequently reflect and review all your major chances, changes and choices in your life each day, month, and year. In order to realize your destiny, you need to step back and assess where you are investing most of your time and energy. Each day you have the opportunity to take serious action toward creating the life and destiny you want. Make a daily choice to empower your life to take a chance and create your destiny.

Taking a chance in life may offer you an opportunity to grow exponentially, open a door that was first unseen, or see the new stepping-stones paving the path to your goals. Attempting a new adventure is being willing to remove yourself outside your comfort zone to pursue your passion and purpose. Taking a chance can mean the difference between a mediocre or a marvelous life.

Your choices can create chances or opportunities for you to make an impact in your life, your family, your community, or your organization. By taking the risk or a calculated chance, you can change your life.

One thing for sure in life is change. Change can be good or it can be bad but change is inevitable in life. As you make choices and take chances you change. You grow, you develop, and you reinvent yourself as you journey in life. In addition, as you change over the years you are not the same person you were as you began your journey. Life would be stagnant and unproductive if you did not grow and change. You are the only one that can make the choice and take the chance to develop yourself and make your lifelong dreams became a reality.

So accept the choice to take the chance to make the change. Change your life today, it all starts with your own choice. This is up to you! Better choices lead to a better chance to change. If you do not make the choice you will never change. Always remember change is a good thing. Change can make you see a different side of the world we live in today! Now step up to the plate. This is all in your hands.

Every choice you make today will not have the power to alter the trajectory of your life, but there are some that will have that power. What choice will you make? Are you willing to take a chance? Will you embrace change? Remember, you have the power to create the life you want!

~THE WAY TO MOVE FORWARD IS TO MOVE FORWARD~

What does it take to move forward in life? One of the key things needed to move forward is to keep moving forward. You have to move forward by moving forward with the ability to focus. Your mind must be clear about what it needs to focus on. There are times when it is critical to focus on what is taking place at that time. My advice is to focus on what is most important or that appears to be the priority. If you do not focus on what is most important; you could be in real trouble in the near or not to distance future.

God does not want us to be stuck in the past. The problem with always focusing on the past is that it hinders us from looking forward. When we focus only on the issues in the past, we fail to concentrate on the objectives we need to accomplish in the present and on the goals we need to complete in the future. When the past is crippling us, we must learn how to move forward in life.

Moving forward in life, also involves the ability to unstick the mind. Sometimes life will deal you a blow that may cause you to become stuck or unmotivated. Instead of standing your ground and lowering your shoulder, you feel like curling up and throwing in the towel. It is at these times that you must put on all your spiritual armor and prepare for battle. One battle at a time! One fight at a time! One war at a time! This is the kind of attitude you need to move forward in life.

Your moving forward is not a challenge, it is a choice! You can move forward steady and slow or fast and furious, but either way, keep moving forward without hesitation or procrastination. Celebrate every small step you make. Move forward away from discouragement and disappointment. Make the decision to release and reset as you live for what you live for. In other words, you will never move forward unless you become angry with where you are.

To move forward means to make a change of place or position with the intention of advancing towards the front. To move on towards your ultimate goal. With that, you have to have a starting point and keep going and make positive progress. You cannot move forward and make things happen unless you are willing to take a chance.

Taking a chance gives you the change needed for you to break the chains of what is keeping you from move pass your past. Walt Disney said, *"Around here we don't look backwards for very long. We keep moving forward, opening up new doors and doing new things."*

In other words, you need to be in a go and grow mode...time waits for no one and the longer you wait, the further behind you get and those doors will close on you. So get out of your own way.

Whatever you believe and conceive, you are worthy of achieving and receiving it. The closer you get to it is when the enemy of your soul will begin putting doubt in your mind by playing the self-limiting tapes that says you are not worthy. Replace these old tapes with a newer one that contains the truth – you are worthy to have your heart's true desire and to keep moving forward by moving forward.

As you move forward, I want to encourage you to move into an attitude and atmosphere of faith. When you feel weary and life continues to feel uncomfortable, the one thing that tells you to keep going; to get up tomorrow and to keep moving forward, is your faith. Honor this and cherish it. Faith is what makes you human. It gives you energy and hope. And if you let it, your faith will deliver you and drive you to wherever you want to go.

As you move forward in life, occasionally look ahead to your next, new and now horizon. The next challenge you see will give you the drive to keep moving forward, onward and upward. Make the commitment to achieve something as you are moving forward. Keep moving forward to discover your true self and begin to live life as God has planned and purposed for you. Move Forward, Onward and Upward with a fistful of focused faith.

~THE POWER OF A SEED~

Do you want to see a miracle? Try this. Take a seed the size of a freckle. Put it under several inches of dirt. Give it enough water, light and fertilizer. And get ready. A mountain will be moved. It does not matter that the ground is a zillion times the weight of the seed. The seed will push it back. Every harvest begins with a small seed. Growth begins with the sowing of the seed.

Every spring, dreamers around the world plant tiny hopes in overturned soil. And every spring, their hopes press against impossible odds and blossom.

Never underestimate the power of a seed. Think about it. A little tiny seed is basically a treasure-chest of DNA, prepared to (in the right circumstances) give birth to any of a variety of beings. In order for your seed to grow, it takes vision. You have to have a vision for and of the end result.

You do not just grab whatever seeds you can get your hands on, throw them around willy-nilly, and hope for the best. Instead, you have to ask yourself what type of life (garden) you want, the purpose you want your life to serve, what you want to grow in your life and how you want your life laid out. In every seed there is a forest. If you have an apple seed, in that apple seed is an apple tree. There is also apples on that apple tree. So in that one seed you really have a forest.

How do you get a forest out of a seed is the question you ask. 'How do I get my vision out of my life?' The first thing you need to do is to deal with the atmosphere or environment. You take the seed, and you put it in the right atmosphere or environment.

Just as you should have a vision for the seeds you plant, you should have a vision for your life.

Planting thought seeds are your key to gaining a better life. Not everyone is going to have world changing ideas and that is okay, but you can affect the world in a small way by changing your own life for the better.

To change your life you first have to know what you want and what you would love to change about your life. So the first thing to think about is what you would change about your life if you could.

Inside of you there is unlimited potential. If you want to tap into your full potential you will need to be in the right atmosphere and environment, surrounded by the right people, nourished emotionally, mentally, physically and spiritually. Over time your true potential and purpose will be unleashed and just like the apple tree in your life will bear fruit.

Keep in mind, you cannot force a seed to grow faster than nature intended it to, and you cannot make trees bear fruit on demand. All you can do is create the best possible conditions for your seeds, plant the right seeds, and give those seeds the care and attention they need. Then, trust that nature will take care of the rest.

Possess the seeds that will bear the fruit that are most important to you. Then, the next year–if you wish–, you can try planting different seeds. You just cannot think about too many things at the same time.

You alone are the farmer and cultivator of your life, and only you can produce beautiful things in abundance. You can create your own happiness, your own success, and your own change! Plant and grow positive, kind, loving seed thoughts to create a better you!

The seed is one part of your universe that gives you a small glimpse into the infinite intelligence behind the creation and the functioning of your world.

So next time you look at and see an apple seed, do it with respect for what that seed is. After all, you came from a seed.

~TAKE THE LIMITS OFF~

You and I have one thing in common: We want to constantly improve our lives and be the best version of ourselves. But unfortunately, many people have lived their lives pretty much the same way for a very long time.

You are capable of making the biggest transformation of your life. Significant and magnificent lasting changes should not take you years. But it means stepping beyond your current way of life and embracing new habits. To create the level of life you ultimately want, you have to change something you do daily.

Your life is your signature creation. It is your duty to live true to yourself, with authenticity. Your life's mission is to express yourself boldly, create what you love and love what you create. It is about expanding and living your vision of yourself—until it is the greatest possible expression of who you are.

Give yourself permission to take your life to the next level. It is time to take the limits off what God can do in your life, through your life and for your life. It is really easy to remain complacent in your comfort zone day after day, month after month and year after year.

Then you look up and before you realize it, ten years has passed you by and you still have not completed your degree or taken that trip that you promised yourself you would take "next year."

Look beyond yourself. Whether you choose to acknowledge it or not, you were created to live a life that is beyond your comfort zone, in pursuing your purpose in life. Consequently, you can only do this if you get outside of things that are familiar, move out of your own way, and become willing to adopt an attitude and desire to not become so content with the content.

It is time for you to take the limits off and walk in your God appointed purpose and plan. When you do, you manifest and discover extraordinary an unknown part of you that is waiting and wanting to come to life. You limit yourself every time you consciously and unconsciously talk yourself out of what you really desire, need and want.

If you truly want all that life has to offer you and you truly want to take the limits off, all you have to do is look in the mirror and there is the person who can and will make that happen for you. So please stop telling yourself that you "cannot" do this or that, and instead of saying "cannot" tell yourself "Who is Going To Stop Me?" Nobody is going to make your dreams become a reality, because it is your dream. So if you want it, quit making excuse and "Go Get It." Remember this, only you can hold yourself back. Only you can stand in your own way.

When you get out of the way, you stop resisting life. The focus shifts from what you do not have to what is here and available. You no longer doubt everything, you receive what life fully offers you. And rather than living in the mind-created past or future, you are available to the simplicity of this now moment.

No one can put a limit on you without your permission. It is time to take the limits off of your life and take your life to the next level. Your destiny, desires and dreams are out there if you have the courage to take hold of them. Wake up each day, regardless of your circumstances, with the mindset that you are one step closer to that divine limitless appointment that God created just for you.

Take the limits off and get out of your own way. You have the ability to experience Abundance, Confidence, Gratitude, Happiness, Joy, Success and so much more in each and every area of your life. Allow It, Experience It and Receive by taking the limits off of your life.

Do not limit your challenges, challenge your limits.

~UNDERSTANDING YOUR LANDSCAPE~

Have you ever thought about the phrase the grass is always greener on the other side of the fence? I think of a cow eating grass perfectly content until she comes to a fence. On the other side of the fence, she sees all of this beautiful green grass. Suddenly the grass on her side of the fence is not good enough. The cow struggles to find a way onto the other side of the fence and lose focus on what she has and focuses on what she does not.

Does that sound familiar? Sure, the grass on the other side of the fence is a little nicer. It has not been trampled on or eaten, but soon the grass on the new side of the fence is trampled and eaten and is no better than the old side. All of this effort was spent to get to the other side of the fence, which in the end does no good.

The hallmark of the "grass is greener syndrome" is the idea that there is always something better that we are missing. So rather than experiencing satisfaction, security and stability in the present environment, the feeling is there is more and better elsewhere, and anything less than ideal would not do. The greener grass syndrome is usually based on fantasy, failures and fear. When this happens, the perception is that there is something else out there that will allow us to have all that we crave, need, value, want and that it will happen on our terms.

Most people go through life looking through the prism of fear and never look at the potential they have or the destiny they may reach. Where you go, your destiny will accompany you. Do not part company with your destiny because it is the anchor in the storm. Your outlook on life will determine your outcome.

In order to fulfill your destiny, you have to make a plan according to God's purposes and stay focused to fulfill that plan. Proverbs 4:25 says, *"Keep your eyes fixed straight ahead."* Do not look to the left or right and be not distracted and spend time or energy on things that are not helping you fulfill your destiny.

To truly understand your landscape, you must first know that you were born on Purpose, with a Purpose and for a Purpose. Your life's purpose is to live to your full potential. That means understanding the needs, seeds and weeds of in your life. You have to nurture and nourish where you are planted in order for you to grow.

Here is the deal, you have to dream big, dig deep and dare to do! Plant yourself deeper for growth and development. Getting better and better until you find yourself ready and prepared for the highest version of your purpose...the why you are here.

You have to explore and experience as you live to improve yourself. Your life has meaning. You are a garden worth the growth. What you grow in your life's "garden" is completely up to you. Pay attention to your harvest...what is right for you now will have developed into something else in a year's time. That also means that you have to excavate the piles of dirt in your life.

In understanding your landscape and getting away from the "grass is greener syndrome, you have to learn how to nurture and nourish your seeds of life so that you are completely satisfied with an internal place of stability, rather spending all of you time pulling the weeds in your external life to compensate for the lack of internal stability

The landscape of your life changes when the thinking develops into being happy in the moment you are currently in. Maybe there is nothing actually wrong with your grass; you just are not looking at it with a grateful heart.

Remember, the grass is not greener on the other side, it is greener where you water it. Take care of YOUR life and learn to grow where you are planted.

RYAN LAMONT JONES is a profound spiritual leader and acclaimed empowerment legend. His approachable and humble 6'9" stature as well as his charismatic, contagious, enthusiastic personality and presence make people take notice. This ordained minister has over 15-years experience as a dynamic nationally respected award-winning, highly sought after Certified Professional Speaker, Performance Improvement Specialist, Author/Writer and Transformational Trainer.

He has dedicated his life to connecting with and empowering students everywhere. He has risen to national prominence as one of the *Top 25 Speakers Shaping the Speaking Profession* with his hard-hitting, high-energy, content-rich and paradigm-shifting presentations. He conducts keynote addresses, breakout sessions, conferences, conventions, retreats, seminars, training programs and workshops for associations, churches, clubs, colleges and universities, groups, organizations, public and private traditional/non-traditional schools.

He is known for using his unique blend of warmth, humor, insight, compassion and down-to-earth charm to deliver interactive and accessible presentations that are passionate, purposeful and powerful.

When you book Ryan, your audience will leave your event knowledgeable, informed and inspired with strategies and practical tools they can use immediately to better understand and improve the effectiveness of their work.

Some of his civic and professional involvement includes being a member of Kappa Alpha Psi Fraternity, Inc.; National Speakers Association; Professional Coaches Alliance; Member Associate of the American Association of Christian Counselors; American Society for Training & Development and currently serves as Brand Ambassador for Celebs Give Back and I Am Helping as well as serves on the Board of Directors for several organizations and foundations.

FROM THE HEART OF OTHERS ABOUT RYAN

"Ryan is a gentle giant whose message inspires and speaks volumes! His passion allows him to connect in a powerful way touching both hearts and heads."
~Bishop Dale C. Bronner, Senior Pastor/Founder

"I am blessed to call you family, but truly honored to call you a dear friend and confidant. I have always known that your presence in this world would impact lives. You have this very unique and gentle way in which you are able to raise the spiritual consciousness of those you meet just by being your authentic self. You are truly one of God's most beautiful creations. I am so excited for you and glad to be able to witness this new chapter in your life. Love you much!"
~Melody Curry, Cousin

"Poised, passionate, and purposed are a few words I'd use to describe Ryan L. Jones. He is a man that utilizes his God-given abilities, gifts, and talents with an intentionality that is unrivaled. Beyond his physical stature, Ryan's presence looms large in any space that he occupies because, with humility, authenticity, and a quiet confidence, he operates in his gifting. Whenever I hear him speak, I am reminded that he is a talented orator, motivator, and transformational leader divinely appointed to be a catalyst that helps people, throughout many walks of life, become their best selves. Ryan is truly a gem!"
~Pastor Terrence Evans

"When speaking about Ryan L. Jones, there are a lot of great things that one can say about him. However, when describing Ryan the best word that I could come up with is "EPITOME." Ryan is the perfect example of a motivational speaker who has the passion and desire to change lives. His speaking comes with power and his presents comes with

humility. Ryan, is one of the most incredible selfless person that we have ever met.
When you hear Ryan L. Jones speak you know that he comes to give true knowledge that will help others see the best in themselves. He is truly on the Top Shelf and Rising!"

~Ms. JJ Fox, MJGMF/Fox Trap Radio

"The first day I met Ryan not only did I notice his height but I felt his spirit. Ryan is my brother and I am so blessed to have him in my life. When he speaks it's powerful, he is empowering, he is inspiring and gives me a lot of wisdom every time we see each other. When you meet Ryan he will leave an impact on your life then you just want to know more about him and what he is about. He is a great role model for anyone and will keep it real with you because he cares. He is always trying to think of ways to help others because that's who he is. I am proud of you and enjoy watching you grow as you continue your journey empowering many lives all over the world."

~Will Hill IIII

"Ryan L. Jones is a powerful, intelligent and humble servant that uses all of his gifts and talents to help hurting people. Ryan also is dedicated to the transformation and empowerment of all of God's people."

~Bryan A. Jones, M. Div., LPC
Owner and Executive Director
The Joshua Generation Care and Consultant Services, LLC

"The day I met Ryan L. Jones, we were at an elementary school and Ryan was being who he is born to be. He was empowering children and keeping them excited with his infectious charisma. In the years since that day, I have only known Ryan to be more of the same. Ryan's personality, style and approach to empowering, exciting and educating others is fresh and always engaging. Only a person who loves and enjoys what he does can inspire so many using the variety of tools in his God given tool box. I am honored to know and be acquainted with such an empowering person. I am not just a friend and a fan, but like so many

others, I am also truly inspired by and through him. Thanks Ryan for being such a powerful role model."
    ~Dave H. Jordan, Relationship Coach/Mentor/Motivator/Author

"Ryan L. Jones is exuberating, inspiring, motivational and convincing! He is a walking testimony for every person that wants to find respect and themselves. Ryan knows how to connect with the heart of people who feel misguided or abandoned by life's circumstances. Mr. Jones is a must-have for energizing hope, pride, spirituality, and determination for all age groups of people. Since I've known Brother Ryan his work, his walk of life and his drive to help others have been consistent."
    ~Tommie Mabry, Author/Chief Executive Officer/Teacher/Motivational Speaker

"To be in position to witness faith in action transform a person's life, it's hard not to be inspired and blessed by the overflow. Ryan L. Jones empowers his listeners, readers, and those around him to experience life awakening concepts that transcends all ages and stages in life."
    ~Shayla "Phriday" Patterson, Actor/Public Relations Consultant

"Ryan Jones is a very intellectual and empowering man. He is an amazing attention grabber and he speaks openly and honestly about the expectations of life. He is very passionate about what he does and he is a powerful influencer. I would highly recommend him to speak as he encourages people to excel in life."
    ~DeShanta Reese

"Ryan is one of the most impactful, influential, and inspiring people that I've ever known! I've been privileged to do life with him for nearly a decade and he is the REAL DEAL! Consistent. Compassionate. A true leader. A natural encourager. This book will not only challenge your head but it'll also stretch the capacity of your heart in the process."
    ~Jason H. Thomas

"Ryan Lamont Jones is someone I consider a good friend. I'm thankful each and every day that we've crossed paths and get to journey through life together. Ryan has a wealth of knowledge and application and he shares with individuals and large crowds every chance he gets. He truly cares about each and every person having the best life that's available to them and he's willing to help them get to it in every way that he can. If there's one man I can trust with my friendship and time it is Ryan."
~Carlos Torres, Oasis Family Life Church

"To know Him and the Power of His Resurrection...is one of my favorite scriptures. After meeting Ryan L. Jones I reflect on this scripture as knowing Ryan and the Power God has given him through speech. Yet, he remains humbled and honored. It only took one meeting for us to know Ryan had to be on air at Vision Radio. The message God has given him is for the masses. It cannot be contained. The Word is like Fire ready to consume everything it contacts. Ryan has a way of teaching the Word to the understanding of the most elementary to the highest scholar. It is a pleasure for me to know him and the Power that lies within him."
~Pastor Owen & Martha Wallace, Owners of WXNV Vision Radio 105.1 FM

"As a Speaker, Minister and Teacher, I make contact with a lot of different people, but Mr. Ryan Jones really is Heaven sent to "US" here on earth. He's a True Servant first of all and he looks for ways to be a blessing to others. I've been given the privilege of watching him make Motivational Speaking look easy, while touching so many lives around the world by his genuineness to stand for change, but most of all, his desire to help save a life."
~Trell "Donk" Webb, Speaker/Minister/Teacher

Ryan L. Jones has been a true gift from God in my life. He literally appeared out of thin air which is hard to do being 6'9, but somehow he did it which speaks directly to his greatness. Honestly Ryan has continually blessed my life with his wisdom, positive outlook, and encouragement. It was so odd for me to have someone who never met me a day in their life speak directly to my heart with real compassion. He has been a true inspiration, and I know that he is inspiring others just as he has done for me. Mr. Jones has a rare gifting to effectively reach, and teach students of all ages no matter what barriers may stand in the way. I know that his new book is going to bless each and every soul that touches it, and I thank God for bringing this brother and mentor into my life. Thank you for speaking life into me brother!!!

~*James Walker*

"Having known Ryan for over 10 years, both professionally and personally, I sit back and wonder 'In what amazing way will GOD use him next!' He is transparent, genuine, and passionate. His character and integrity compel him, effortlessly, to treat the janitor in the exact manner he treats the CEO – with dignity and respect. His message to everyone, not just youth, is inspiring, timeless, and much needed in this day. I am challenged every day to be a better person for having met Ryan."

~*April W. Welch, Assistant Director/ Dean of Students*

"Ryan is a born leader who speaks for this generation and generations to come."

~*Dr. Myles Munroe, Founder/President*

ON THE BACK COVER

I had the pleasure of meeting Tommy Ford in 2015 at a local high school. We instantly connected and a week later over lunch, and it became evident that he and I would become "unconditional" brothers and friends. I am always grateful for him telling me that our "job" is to be about doing God's business. He and I shared our vision to give back to the community and share ourselves with others. His love for us will always and in all ways be felt. I am grateful for him allowing my path to cross with other people who have the same spirit that Tommy possessed. Because of our relationship, I will always have a job to do. (Thank you Dawg, and I love you my brother. RIH).

I am so damn grateful for Kimberly Hawthorne, Mark Christopher Lawrence and Jazsmin Lewis-Kelley; I am truly humbled and honored to have them in my life. I have been blessed to see them in their craft on television, movies or on stage, but beyond that, they all possess a humility, gratitude and down-to-earth spirit that is as genuine and pure. What I LOVE about each of them, is that, none of them made or allowed their "celebrity" to dominate them, but their connection to people did and always does.

The words they shared about me, I can truly say the same about each of them. Not one time, have you not answered my phone call or responded to a text or email.

Thank you Kim, Mark and Jazsmin for empowering me on this journey. As a reflection of each of you, let us continue to be "A Season of Change" for the people that we connect with. I love you.

Kimhawthorne.space
Markchristopherlawrence.com
Jazsminlewis.com

Entrepreneur/Pastor/On-Air Personality/Life Coach /Mentor/Consultant/Adjunct Professor

Email: ryan@rljonesandassociates.net

Social media: **@standtallryan**